FIG. 2. Play clothes are essential for every child.

Play Clothes Influence Development of Child

No child's clothing outfit is complete until it contains adequate garments for good wholesome play. If children have suitable play clothing they will be encouraged to play more; they will thoroly enjoy their play and not be handicapped with the fear that mother will scold if they get dirty or torn. (Fig. 2). Suitable clothing will be a definite saving on the school and dress-up clothes altho these should never be too good for some kinds of play. Children can be encouraged to take better care of their other clothing when they know that there is clothing provided for rough play. Play clothes may be attractive as well as useful.

1. Coveralls make a satisfactory play garment. In the summer they may be worn with very little other clothing underneath them. During cooler weather and winter it is a splendid idea to have coveralls large enough to be worn over the sweater or coat and thereby protect garments more difficult to clean.

2. Rompers, aprons and simple play dresses are useful for play garments.

3. Adequate provision should be made for wraps for play; those which are too small should never be used for they may be a handicap to development.

4. Sweaters are good for general wear for both boys and girls; they give warmth and allow freedom of movement.

5. Good rubbers, overshoes, mittens and warm caps are an insurance against unnecessary exposure. The knitted helmet type of cap protects the ears, chin and throat during cold weather. Rubber overshoes are preferable to those made of heavy cloth because they are waterproof and more easily cleaned.

6. Leggings to be pulled on are more satisfactory than those which must be carefully fitted and buttoned and unbuttoned each time they are worn.

Clothes Influence Character

Many points favor clothing which is attractive yet which make a child absolutely unconscious of them. (1) The garment must be simple, comfortable and of material not easily soiled. (2) A child over-dressed in extravagant, fussy, or faddish clothing can not be natural and is apt to think too much about clothes and to become snobbish and affected. (3) One who is oddly or unattractively dressed is as self-conscious as is one who has to wear clothes which are much too large or too small for him. (4) A child dressed in ragged clothing is slovenly and will not have self-respect. (5) Adequate, attractive, simple, appropriate, clean and comfortable clothes will help to keep the child from being self-conscious, improve his disposition, cultivate genuiness and establish ideals.

Clothes and Behavior

Teachers and mothers find that clothing seems to exert a decided influence on the behavior of the child, strange as it may seem. (Fig. 7). Therefore, we are reminded again that clothes must be chosen with the greatest of care. Men and women are more or less slaves to public opinion in matters of dress and you will usually find that this same old bogy exerts a similar power over a child. Your child may dislike school because of some ridiculed garment which he is made to wear, one that is too "different" from those of the other children, one that is not masculine enough for your small boy, or clothes that are too large or too small.

FIG. 3. Clothes which suit the personality of the child encourage good behavior.

Children's work or play may be greatly affected from just such things for neither a child nor a grown-up can think clearly with a harassed mind.

Do not think of your child's dislike for certain clothes as unimportant for it is important to the child and it may make his days nightmares of dread and shame and thereby affect his disposition, behavior, and health. Children are cruel to their playmates for they have not yet acquired the veneer of courtesy. With an uncanny instinct they find the sore spots in their play-

CLOTHES

FOR LITTLE FOLKS

IOWA STATE COLLEGE
OF AGRICULTURE AND MECHANIC ARTS
Extension Service
R. K. Bliss-Director
Ames-Iowa

Cooperative Extension Work
in Agriculture and Home Economics

*Iowa State College of Agriculture and Mechanic Arts and the
United States Department of Agriculture,
cooperating*

DISTRIBUTED IN FURTHERANCE OF THE ACTS OF CONGRESS OF MAY 8
AND JUNE 30, 1914

CLOTHES FOR LITTLE FOLKS

By MILDRED B. ELDER
Illustrated by Irma Camp Graff

Children's clothes exert such a decided influence upon their health and happiness that they should have the most thoughtful attention. The individual garment must be suited to the best development of the body, mind and character. Too often style or fashion are followed without reason and common sense when the first consideration should be for the comfort of the child.

Clothing and Health

1. Clothes should be loose enough to permit plenty of activity which gives the body an unrestricted opportunity to grow.
2. There should be complete and even covering of the body.
3. Provision should be made for warm clothing for winter so that there will be adequate protection from cold.
4. In warm weather select cool clothes and those which allow sunlight to reach the skin directly.
5. Improper clothing may interfere with circulation, breathing, or digestion; it may cause round shoulders, weaken muscles, distort feet, cause nervousness, increase susceptibility to colds, and displace certain organs.
6. Play helps children to develop strong healthy bodies, and all clothes should be planned to make wholesome play possible. (Fig. 1).
7. Shoes and stockings should be comfortably fitted. Never use outgrown shoes.
8. Hose supporters which will hang from or be supported from the shoulders should be selected. If there is a strain on the shoulders caused by supporters which are placed toward the front or if supporters are too short, round shoulders are apt to result.
9. Knee joints should be protected, except in warm weather.
10. Tight bands or elastics which restrict circulation must never be used.

FIG. 1. Clothes which allow active play help to develop robust, healthy children.

5

mates and laugh and tease without a thought or care for the misery which they may cause their victim. Childish heart-aches and hot-rebellion often results and we are at loss to know just what is the trouble. At any rate we should analyse the clothing and make sure it is all right.

"Dressy" or feminine clothes on little boys mean martyrdom to most of them. Little girls like to be attractively and neatly dressed. When they are very young they may be encouraged to form habits of cleanliness and care of their clothing which will make lasting habits. Clothing should not be too large for the child. Such clothing makes him appear at a disadvantage. When only an adequate supply of clothes are provided they are worn out before they are out-grown. This, of course, does not mean that the rapid growth of the child should not be provided for but it can usually be done so that the garment will not look extreme in its provision for it.

Hygienic Clothing

Health and hygiene are closely related. Frequent laundering is the best assurance that clothes are kept as hygienic as possible.
1. No garment should be selected for a young child unless it can be laundered or cleaned.
2. Wash materials are most hygienic and satisfactory.
3. An adequate number of garments in the wardrobe means that frequent changes can be made.
4. When garments are color-fast and simple in design they may be easily laundered and are apt to be kept more hygienic than when there is a dread about the laundry problem.
5. Children gain self-respect and poise when kept clean.

Economy Should be Practiced

Careful thought and planning on the part of the mother will assure her of economy in the expenditure of money, time and energy and she must try to make the best possible plans. Determining factors will usually be (1) the amount of the family income (2) the number of children to provide clothing for, (3) the health of the mother, (4) the available time that may be spent on clothing and (5) the enjoyment which the mother may get from this particular phase of her home problem.

Economy of Time and Energy

1. The clothing problem should be simplified so it will not take an unjust amount of the mother's time and energy.
2. The amount of the family budget will often decide whether garments should be made by the mother. If her health deems it unwise to make clothes they should be bought ready-made or made by some one else even tho the cost is greater.
3. It is well to study carefully which garments are best to buy and to make. Ready made sleeping garments, play suits and underwear are usually very satisfactory.
4. Simple designs and patterns with as few pieces as possible should be chosen.

5. Using foundation patterns with which one is thoroly familiar saves time in making a garment.
6. Garments which can be ironed flat or quickly simplify laundering.
7. The use of machine attachments means efficiency of time in construction.
8. Clothing made loose and large enough with provision for altering to take care of the rapid growth of the child is an economy.
9. Two pair of trousers for little boys' suits will often save laundering an entire suit and a shirt will always outwear one pair of trousers.
10. Protecting clothing such as aprons and bibs and giving all garments good care will prolong their service and thus save time and energy in replacing them.

Economy of Money

Most mothers find there is economy in providing three types of clothing for each child, one for dress-up occasion, church and social affairs, one for school and one distinctly for play and home wear. If the time and place to wear each outfit is respected there should be a definite savings in the clothing budget.

1. When the mother is capable of getting satisfactory results and enjoys sewing there is considerable economy in making garments.
2. Good quality, durable and color-fast materials are an economy even tho the initial cost is greater.
3. Choose patterns which require minimum amounts of material and those that cut to good advantage.
4. Cheap ready-made garments are usually not an economy in the long run.
5. Inexpensive trimmings and finishes can be made from bias-tape, decorative stitches, buttons, etc.
6. Sizes which allow for rapid growth should be selected.
7. "Made-over" clothing often saves the cost of a new garment.
8. Buy several pairs of stockings of the same kind and color so that pairs may be re-mated according to the amount of wear they show.

Artistic and Attractive Clothes

Realizing that clothes should be more than a covering and protection to the body we strive to have them artistic and attractive; they give more satisfaction to those who see them as well as to those who wear them. Children are no less sensitive to this than grown-ups, in fact, at times clothes seem to have a greater effect on their health, happiness, development, and behavior than we are apt to realize.

Clothing which is becoming emphasizes the best characteristics in both face and body and will take only a little added thot when planning to be assured that this can be said of children's clothing. Becomingness brings out individuality and personality which makes the child more attractive. (Fig. 3).

Becoming Designs

1. Design principles should be applied to children's garments and are the same as grown-ups.
2. Study the type of figure deciding whether child is taller or broader than the average and which lines are the best ones to emphasize and which defects must be concealed.

FIG. 4. Width, lines and fullness make the figure appear wider and are becoming for slender children.

3. Width lines and a noticeable amount of fullness or gathers add width to the figure and make the thin child appear broader and not so thin. (Fig. 4).
4. Length is apparently gained when simplicity and tailored effects are used and when vertical (length) lines are predominant. (Fig. 5).
5. Lines can easily be emphasized on girl's clothing but is a little difficult on little boy's clothing, however, designs for their clothing should be analysed for the effect of line.
6. Suits which are of all one color will not cut the figure and apparently shorten as much as those which show a contrast in the color or material used for the shirt and trousers. (Fig. 4).
7. Large plaids and large figured or spotty materials seem to increase size and are not in proportion to the child's figure.
8. Stripes seemingly lengthen the figure while tiny checks or small all-over figured materials and those of solid color seem to leave the figure unchanged as far as length or width is concerned.
9. Heavy fabrics, sturdy stripes, tailored styles and those free from fussiness or trimming seem appropriate for the little boy.

FIG. 5. Length lines and tailored effects slenderize the short or broad child.

10. A large variety of wash materials in various types and weaves are suitable for little girls' clothing. Hand stitches and dainty trimmings of braids and bias tape are effective finishes for them.

11. The type of the child often determine just what the definite choice shall be. The athletic, vivacious child looks well in garments which would be quite unbecoming to the quaint, dainty demure type.

Becoming Colors

1. Becoming colors are those which bring out attractively the good points in the personal coloring of the wearer. This means that the coloring of the child should be studied and considered when planning clothing.

2. The color of the hair, eyes, or skin may be greatly enhanced when the right color is used.

3. There is a bewildering lot of attractive colored fabrics that are lovely for children but it is not true that a child can wear *any* color, tho they have a greater number of becoming ones than the average grown-up, due mostly to their own vivid and clear coloring and their clear skin.

4. The fair-complexioned, golden haired, blue eyed child may wear a large variety of colors, all shades of blues are good, and pinks, greens, and lavenders are usually becoming. The lighter values of the colors seem suited to this type.

5. The child with dark skin, brown hair and eyes will do well to wear the richer deeper shades of the colors for they will seem more appropriate than the delicate ones. Cream yellow, orange, brown, red and greens are attractive.

6. The child with auburn hair, fair skin and blue or brown eyes will look best in browns, grey-blues, blue-greens, greens, dull orange and lavender and they never find reds or pinks becoming.

Colors Should Suit the Personality of the Child

1. Be careful not to subdue the personality of the child by using too bright a color or too large an amount of it. One must keep in mind the disposition or type of child in planning colors.

2. Bright reds and other conspicuous colors used for a bashful, self-conscious child may cause him to feel more ill at ease.

3. Soft, rich and duller (tho not drab) colors will be more becoming and will make children feel less conscious of themselves.

4. Dainty and rich colors are suited to the dainty child while more daring, clear colors will be suitable for the athletic, vivacious child.

5. For little boy's clothing be sure to choose colors which seem masculine. There is a wider range to choose from for young boys than for older boys for they soon learn to resent wearing ''girlish'' colors.

Considerations in Color Choices

1. Keep in mind a definite color scheme for the entire outfit so that hats, coats, dresses, suits, shoes and stockings will blend in color and make a harmonious and pleasing whole.

2. Colors delight children and seem to make them happy. It is worthwhile to encourage and indulge children in enjoying color for it gives them pleasure to possess clothing of their favorite color.

3. Often if the child's color preference is satisfied he takes pride in appearing his very best and in that way develops habits of care and respect for his clothing.

4. Mothers are fortunate now in being able to buy almost every fabric with a color-fast guarantee on it. Because of this they need never hesitate about choosing lovely colors for the children's garments.

5. Clothing made from color-fast materials insure one against having faded, ugly garments. They do not necessitate special care in laundering.

FIG. 6. Under garments and hose supporters need the most careful selection.

Undergarments

Undergarments need even more careful consideration for the child than for the adult. So much energy is necessary for growth that every bit possible must be conserved. This may be partially accomplished when undergarments are wisely chosen.

1. Loosely woven or knitted material is best for underwear for it gives opportunity for ventilation which aids in the evaporation of perspiration.
2. Cotton is most desirable for it is warm, durable, easily laundered, light in weight and inexpensive.
3. White undergarments will always look well and may be kept more hygienic for they can be boiled.
4. Union garments are best for they distribute the weight of the garment evenly on the shoulders. (Fig. 6).
5. In buying or making garments be sure they are plenty large, that the crotch is wide, the armholes deep and the seat generous.
6. Select garments with flat, smooth seams, strong edge finishes and strong buttonholes.
7. Straps on undergarments should be two or three inches wide so that the weight is across the entire shoulder.
8. Waist line of the garment should measure from four to seven inches larger than that of the child.
9. Garments with reinforcing tapes for supporters and buttons eliminate the need of underwaists.
10. Front closing garments are most easily fastened by children.
11. Buttons at waistline of underwaist may be used to adjust length of bloomers or trousers.
12. Taped on buttons make strong fastenings and are easily managed by children.
13. Several layers of light, loosely woven fabrics give more warmth than one layer of extremely heavy underwear.

Bloomers

1. Bloomers matching the dress give a neat appearance.
2. Select or make bloomers which are sufficiently deep in the crotch to assure comfort. Unless this care is taken, not only annoyance, irritation and discomfort will result, but often habits may be established which will eventually undermine the health and morals. Mothers cannot be too careful in avoiding these dangers.
3. Allow ample length from waistline to crotch and ample leg width. These precautions will usually prevent the garment from tearing.
4. Patterns which are straight in front and allow for pleats or gathers on the side seam of the back fit and wear well.
5. Belts and bands should be used instead of tight elastic.
6. Waist bands should be from four to seven inches larger than the waist measure.
7. Pleats in the band for width and a tuck between the waist and crotch will allow for lengthening in case of rapid growth.
8. Three strong button holes in back and front bands are sufficient.
9. Mark front with colored stitch or make band of another color.
10. Leg band should be large enough to push up several inches above the knee. (If a pleat is stitched into the band it may be easily enlarged.)
11. Bloomers sewed onto an underwaist hang well and the length is easily adjusted when a tuck is placed at the waist. This saves making and fastening buttonholes in front. It also means there is no chance of garments coming apart at the waistline.
12. Flat felled seams are most satisfactory. Extension bound plackets are good. Crotch should be made double.

Hose Supporters and Garters

1. Hose-supporters should hang from or be supported from the shoulders. However, if too great a strain is on the shoulders round shoulders and poor posture may result.
2. Supporters should be fastened to underwaists on the side, rather than the front so that the strain is divided between the back and front.
3. Separate supporters which hang from the shoulders are satisfactory when made simply so that the parts do not become easily tangled. (Fig. 6).
4. Hose-supporters should be long enough to adjust carefully to the height of the child. Elastic which has lost its stretch should be replaced immediately.
5. For boys wearing long trousers shaped garters (like men's) are best.
6. Round garters made from elastic should not be used. When tight enough to hold up stockings they are usually tight enough to restrict the circulation of the blood.
7. If elastic must be used for short socks be sure it is loose enough to leave no mark on the body. (Select socks with tightly woven tops which stay in place when folded back without elastic).
8. Several pair of supporters should be provided so that frequent changes may be made.

Shoes

Almost all children are born with perfect feet. Foot defects with which many adults are handicapped are caused from wearing the wrong kind of shoes. It behooves us then to be extremely careful in selecting shoes for children. Always be sure they are sufficiently large and long enough to permit freedom of movement and that they are discarded as soon as they seem short and uncomfortable. Wearing out-grown shoes, as well as other garments is very injurious to the best development of the child.

Stockings

1. Stockings should measure one-half inch longer than the child's foot. This should be the guide for buying rather than size numbers.
2. Cotton is the most suitable fiber for children's hosiery. Lisle, silk and wool are sometimes used.
3. Ribbed stockings are always most suitable for children.
4. It is most economical if several pair of stockings of the same kind and color are bought. When they become worn badly they may then be mated according to their condition.
5. Hose supporters should be fastened carefully so that the top of stocking is not torn.
6. Short socks are attractive for warm weather but should not be worn in cold seasons. Select those with closely knitted tops which help to keep them in place.

Sleeping Garments

1. One-piece sleepers may be bought ready made or made at home. In either case they should be large and roomy. These (Fig. 7) are most satisfactory for younger children.
2. Knitted cotton materials, outing flannel or muslin may be used for night gowns or pajamas.
3. Garments may be made with feet attached for young children and drawstrings in the hem of the sleeves so that the hands may be covered.
4. A garment may be lengthened by inserting a piece in the waist.

FIG. 7. Sleeping garments should be roomy and comfortable.

5. Short sleeved muslin gowns may be used for summer for older girls.
6. One or two-piece pajamas are satisfactory for older boys.

Dresses

1. Choose becoming designs, colors and materials. (Fig. 8).
2. Select appropriate wash materials.
3. Choose simple patterns and those in as few pieces as possible.
4. Raglan and kimona sleeved patterns and those with fullness across the chest are most comfortable and not quickly outgrown.
5. Be sure that arm holes, neck bands, and cuff bands are comfortably loose.
6. One or two foundation patterns may be varied in different ways and used for several dresses.
7. French or plain seams are best for most materials.

8. Hems should be at least five inches to allow for lengthening. Hand hemming shows less and is more easily ripped when length must be changed.
9. Avoid elaborate and fussy trimmings and those which will not launder well.
10. Use darts on the side seam under the arm or under belt if seam sags or if dress draws up in front.
11. Stitchery in lovely colors adds individuality and makes attractive trimmings.
12. Collar and cuffs, pockets and belts when cleverly planned serve as trimmings.
13. All parts of dress must be stitched securely and effects which might quickly become shabby should be avoided.

Boys' Clothing

1. Clothes for boys should be as masculine as possible and be suited to the activities which they enjoy.
2. Design and color principles should be applied to boys clothing.
3. Heavy wash materials and wool fabrics are suitable.
4. Stripes and plain colored fabrics seem best adapted to boyish clothes rather than figured or plaid ones.
5. Suits for little boys are usually made in two pieces with trousers buttoning on waist or blouse hanging loosely over the top of the trousers.
6. Tailored effects such as rows of stitching, bindings, and buttons should be used for trimmings.
7. Older boys usually wear shirts and trousers. Wool sweaters are very satisfactory.
8. Short trousers allow more freedom than long ones and are more easily cleaned and mended. Do not choose heavy or stiff material for them.
9. Use carefully fitted belts or suspender waist for keeping trousers in place.

Coats

1. Materials for coats need not be heavy and bulky to give warmth. Those that are loosely woven and light in weight should be chosen.
2. Linings give added warmth because of the air space between them and the coat materials.
3. Coats should not be stiff or heavy for they give unnecessary strain on the shoulders and create poor posture.
4. Raglan sleeved coats give ample width across the shoulders, allowing freedom of movement and rapid growth.
5. Armholes should be large and roomy. Collars are made comfortably loose and not high enough to push the head forward.
6. Neutral colors or those which blend with other clothing should be chosen for coats.
7. Pockets, large buttons and buttonholes are needed on every coat.

Sweaters

1. Sweaters are essential for every child's wardrobe. They give added warmth under a coat and provide a light weight wrap.
2. Sweaters give warmth and yet are light in weight and allow freedom of movement.
3. Coat sweaters serve as a wrap for children of all ages.
4. Slip-on sweaters may be used as a wrap and also serve as part of school costume for both boys and girls. (Fig. 5).

FIG. 8. Becoming and attractive clothes encourage self-confidence and influence character building.

Hats and Caps

1. Select hats and caps with soft head bands comfortably loose.
2. A brim of some kind is a protection to the eyes.
3. Use soft becoming brim finishes around the face for girls.
4. Select colors with regard for personal coloring as well as parts of a costume.
5. Simple hats without elaborate trimmings are more appropriate and durable.
6. Hats for little boys and girls may be easily made from heavy wash materials or wool. These may be made to match the suit, coat or dress.
7. Satisfactory hats for girls are made from durable soft straws, felt, silk, velvet, wool and wash materials.
8. Knitted caps are good for wear during cold weather.

Precautions in Clothing Selection Which Allows for Growth of Child

1. Buy sleeping garments several sizes larger than that which the child measures.
2. Select patterns and clothing which gives ample fullness across the shoulders and those which have large roomy armholes.
3. Buy patterns and clothing by measurements of the child rather than his age.
4. Be sure suits, undergarments and bloomers are several inches larger at the waistline than exact measurement of the child.
5. Underwear, sleeping garments, suits and other one-piece garments may be made with deep tuck thru the waist to allow for length.
6. At least five inch hems should be used on dresses.
7. Bloomers should be made with a tuck across the top so that length from crotch to waist may be altered when needed.
8. Boy's trousers should be made long enough to turn the hem up twice so they may be lengthened easily.
9. Boys shirts or blouses may be lengthened when a blind tuck has been made across the lower part of them.
10. Make waist bands from four to seven inches larger than the measurement of the child.

FIG. 9.   Closets should be arranged so children can hang up their own clothing.

Construction Which Develops Self-reliance in Dressing

1. Use garments which hang from the shoulder and those with few buttons and openings.
2. Choose sleeping garments, and underwear with a front opening.
3. Make front plackets in dresses and suits.
4. Use fairly large buttons sewed on with a shank of thread or tape.

5. Loop buttonholes and those that are large are most easily fastened by the child.
6. Use as few fastenings as possible. Garments which slip over the head should be used whenever possible. (Sweater, underwaist, and slips).
7. Mark bloomers with a colored thread on the front band or make band of white so that child may recognize front of garment easily.
8. Make boys trousers with as few buttons as possible.
9. Do not use fly in front of small boys trousers. Drop fronts are more easily adjusted.
10. Laced shoes are managed easily by children. Keep tips of laces in repair.
11. Turn stockings wrong side out except for heel. They may then be easily put onto the foot and drawn up over the leg.

Care of Childrens' Clothing

Good habits in the care of clothing should be established in children at a very early age. It will help make them appear well-groomed and will be a definite saving on the clothing which they wear. Frequent baths and clean clothes create self-respect and a natural desire to keep one's self well-groomed.

If a mother expects and insists on care of clothes the children usually acquire these good habits and time and effort spent in training young children will save many efforts in later years. Often by praising the child who is naturally orderly, neatness may be encouraged in other children. A word of praise always is appreciated when a child does take good care of his clothing, in fact, appealing to a child's pride, often is one of the best methods of training.

1. Enough changes in all clothing, especially undergarments should be provided so that cleanliness is assured.
2. It is well to have three distinct outfits (1) one for social and church occasions (2) one for school (3) and one for play.

FIG. 10. Lower drawer space should be used for children's garments.

3. A definite distinction should be made between play and dress clothes. Children usually learn by example and if parents are careful of their own clothing children are apt to acquire good clothing habits.
4. Changing to play-suits, home dresses, and aprons after school is a decided saving on school clothes.
5. Plenty of clean handkerchiefs as well as bibs and napkins help save clothing.
6. At an early age children can be taught to hang clothes in place if there is a definite hook for each garment. (Fig. 9).
7. Hooks and shelves placed low enough for the child to reach will leave no excuse for finding garments out of place. (These should be both up and down stairs).

3. A definite distinction should be made between play and dress clothes. Children usually learn by example and if parents are careful of their own clothing children are apt to acquire good clothing habits.

4. Changing to play-suits, home dresses, and aprons after school is a decided saving on school clothes.

5. Plenty of clean handkerchiefs as well as bibs and napkins help save clothing.

6. At an early age children can be taught to hang clothes in place if there is a definite hook for each garment. (Fig. 9).

7. Hooks and shelves placed low enough for the child to reach will leave no excuse for finding garments out of place. (These should be both up and down stairs).

8. When there are several children in the family it is often helpful to have the child's name pasted near the hook so it will belong distinctly to him.

9. Wall bags made with numerous pockets hung in an inconspicuous place often solve the problem of taking care of little shoes, bedroom slippers, mittens and such things. Names may be placed on these pockets.

10. Small hangers are a splendid investment for they keep the little garments in good condition and require less space for storing. (Fig. 14).

11. Lower drawer space for children's clothing can be partitioned off into distinct spaces which simplify the storage problem and help to have garments kept in order. (Fig. 10).

12. When children have a definite part in choosing and buying clothing they usually take better care of them because they realize their value.

BABY CLOTHES

IOWA STATE COLLEGE
OF AGRICULTURE AND MECHANIC ARTS
Extension Service
R. K. Bliss-Director
Ames-Iowa

Cooperative Extension Work
in Agriculture and Home Economics
Iowa State College of Agriculture and Mechanic Arts and the
United States Department of Agriculture,
cooperating

BABY CLOTHES

By Mildred B. Elder

Illustrated by Irma Camp Graff

Modern baby clothes when compared to those of a generation or so ago show as radical a change as any other clothing. If reasons were found for this they would probably be based upon the same conclusion which women have reached in regard to other clothing matters, that simple, comfortable and attractive garments are more healthful, sanitary and becoming. Clothes of this type assure efficiency of time and energy in making and laundering. The consideration of saving the time and energy of the mother is especially essential when planning baby clothes. When simplicity is the keynote of the entire layette she may count on having more time and strength for other matters of importance.

Since "Clothes were made for babies, not babies for clothes," the baby's welfare must be considered first and the costly coat, too elaborate to be washed easily, and the expensive dress which is over-trimmed will be replaced by more common-sense garments in which the baby will be more comfortable and contented and look just as well.

Doctors, nurses and infant welfare workers encourage simplicity in baby clothing and stress the fact that the baby's health and happiness should be the first consideration.

For the first few months the clothes problem is comparatively simple and rather than provide too many it is well to have a very conservative supply in the beginning. Be sure to have a large supply of diapers and underwear for they are the essentials. Three or four slips, dresses, wrappers and nightgowns are needed and dresses may be used for special occasions but the baby may better be kept in simple slips for the first few months.

Babies should never be dressed or covered so warmly that they perspire or so lightly that they become chilled. The thickness and amount of underclothing should depend largely upon the season of the year and the climate. None of the clothing should be heavy or stiff. It is better to dress babies lightly and use an extra jacket for cool mornings or evenings. Prickly heat may be caused by too much clothing or by wool clothing next to the skin as well as by hot weather. Colds often result from

Fig. 1. Simplicity is the keynote of modern baby clothes.

exposure after a baby has been perspiring, due to an excess amount of clothing.

Those who have studied the matter very carefully feel that no wool garments should be used next to the delicate and tender skin of the young baby. Reports from the Children's Bureau advise the use of cotton for babies' garments for winter and summer. A loose mesh cotton fabric is as warm as wool of the same weight, much less irritating to the baby's tender skin, less expensive and can be boiled and easily laundered.

Extra warmth may be gained by using several layers of clothing rather than heavy, bulky garments.

Essentials in Planning Clothing for Babies

Several important considerations need to be kept in mind in planning baby garments which are as follows:
1. Simple garments are more suitable and attractive.
2. Garments must be sufficiently loose to permit freedom of movement and assure ease in dressing the baby. (Large armholes and long plackets are a great help.)
3. Materials must be soft, dainty and washable.
4. No wool should be used next to the baby's tender skin.
5. Seams, hems, trimmings and all finishes should be flat, smooth and soft so that they will not irritate the sensitive skin of the baby.
6. Suitable trimmings may be made with tiny tucks, decorative stitches and simple embroideries.

Number of Garments

A sufficient number of garments should be prepared for the baby so that frequent changes may be made without causing the mother worry over the need of immediate laundering, altho, of course, whenever possible laundry should be done daily. When too many garments are provided they are outgrown before they are worn out and must be replaced by larger sizes. The amount of money to be spent on the layette will often determine to some extent the quality and number of garments to be made. When care is used in planning and making the cost of the layette should be small. Garments that are most essential should be prepared first.

Approved Garments

1. Front closing shirt.
2. Back closing slip, dresses, and night gowns.
3. Front closing kimona wrapper or sack.
4. Gertrude petticoat fastening on the shoulders.
5. Baby bunting with sleeves.

Simple patterns should always be chosen for these garments, those cut in as few pieces as possible and those that require minimum effort in making and laundering.

The Layette

3 cotton shirts open down front (size No. 2)
3 cotton abdominal bands
3 pair cotton stockings (size No. 4)
2 pair wool bootees (knitted or crocheted)
4 outing gowns
3 outing gertrudes
2 dresses
4 thin slips
3 thin gowns for summer
4 dozen diapers (18x36 inches)
                (22x44 inches)
                (27x54 inches)
2 knitted or crocheted wool jackets
2 kimona wrappers
1 baby bunting
3 bibs

---

3 outing blankets (each 36x36 inches)
2 wool blankets for baby bed
4 muslin sheets for baby bed
1 draw sheet made from flannelette rubberized sheeting
1 mattress cover of table-felting or bath toweling enclosed in pillow slip
3 soft cotton wash cloths (cheese cloth)
3 old soft towels

Materials for Garments

Dresses or Slips	Nightgowns	Kimona Wrappers
Nainsook	Outing flannel	Outing flannel
Muslin	Canton flannel	Albatross
Cambric	Muslin (for summer)	Challis
Lawn	Cambric	Cashmere
Batiste	**Bibs**	
Dimity	Linen Batiste	**Bootees and Jackets**
Flaxon	Muslin Pique	Wool yarn

Measurements for Dresses, Night Gowns and Petticoats

Neck 10-12½ inches
Armhole 9 inches
Wrist 5-6 inches
Sleeve length 6 inches
Placket 8 inches
Length finished
Dresses 20-24 inches
Night gowns 27-30 inches

Chest 34 inches
Shoulder 2¾ plus ½ inch
for tucks or plaits
Hem 2 or 3 inches
Bottom width of skirt 40
inches

CONSTRUCTION OF GARMENTS

Seams must be free from bulkiness. Kimonas, night gowns, and gertrudes should be made with flat felled seams. Small french seams are daintiest for dresses and slips. Garments of heavy material such as flannel require plain wide seams with raw edges, catch stitched down at each side. Seams are most satisfactory when stitched on the machine.

Hems should be flat and wide so they will not form a bulky roll or ridge. They may be hand hemmed or finished with a simple decorative stitch.

Trimmings made with tiny hand-run tucks with fine feather-stitching between them are attractive. Smocking, chain-stitch, blanket stitch, simple embroideries and tiny lace may be used.

Color if used on baby garments should be the daintiest shades of blue and pink. White garments and trimmings are most appropriate and satisfactory.

Diapers

Diapers are one of the most important articles of the baby's clothing, and therefore should be given special thought. Many advise that no baby should start his career in life with less than four dozen diapers. Oblong diapers have more possibilities for changing the size as the child grows. One dozen of the first size, 18x36 inches, and three dozen of the second size, 27x54 inches, provide an adequate supply.

Material

The best grade of outing flannel and cotton bird'seye seem to be the favored materials used and many mothers consider it well to have some made of each of the two materials for they both have their advantages.

Outing flannel keeps soft and is perhaps more easily laundered. It seems to absorb the moisture more readily without becoming saturated and therefore is satisfactory for night wear. Its soft fuzzy finish seems warmer than cotton bird'seye. Bird'seye has a porous weave, which provides good evaporation and ventilation when used for diapers. It can be put onto the baby very neatly and appears less bulky than outing. Because of its weave and finish it makes a cooler garment. All diaper material should be *shrunken before* being cut and hemmed.

Folding

The consensus of doctors, nurses, and mothers is that diapers folded in small triangles during the first two or more weeks are satisfactory and easily pinned in place. After that time the diaper should be folded in an oblong, bringing one end between the legs and arranging the pins at the sides. There is thus less pressure on the organs, more protection and warmth where it is needed, more freedom for exercise and greater comfort for the child. When the diaper is arranged in this way it will appear neater and is much less bulky between the baby's legs.

Rubber pants should only be used on special occasions when such protection is necessary. They hold in heat and do not allow free evaporation of the covered part of the body which may cause irritation. The rubber should never be allowed to touch the skin of the baby and the elastics should not be tight.

Fig. 2. Diapers should be arranged to assure comfort and allow freedom for exercise.

7

Fig. 3. Launder clothes carefully and dry out of doors when possible.

Laundering Baby Clothes

The laundering problem is closely allied to the clothes problem for infants. The garments require frequent and careful washing if they are to be kept sweet and clean. The work is lessened and results are better if the garments are soaped with a mild soap and soaked in luke-warm water for an hour or two before washing. Do not use lye or any strong alkalies in washing such clothing, or too hot, as stains may be set. Tepid water and soap loosen the dirt and less rubbing will be required. Boiling in soap suds usually takes out remaining stains and kills bacterial deposits which may be present. Several thoro rinsings in clean water and drying out of doors in the sun whenever possible will do much to keep the garments sweet and clean.

Wool garments should be washed in castile or Ivory soap suds in tepid water with a little borax or ammonia to soften it. They should be rinsed in water of the same temperature and be squeezed rather than wrung out. Woolens should be dried where there is neither extreme heat or cold if they are to be kept white and soft.

Soiled diapers should never be allowed to dry. They should be washed immediately to remove the stains, and put into water to soak until time for the daily diaper wash. They should be washed in hot soap suds, then boiled for 20 minutes, after which thoroly rinsed. Soap remaining in diapers is liable to cause irritation. No soda, starch or bluing should ever be used in laundering diapers. They should be dried as smoothly as possible out-of-doors when weather permits. They should never be put onto the baby until perfectly dry nor used a second time without careful laundering for they may cause chafing of the baby's tender skin.

Suggestions to be Remembered for Baby Clothes

1. Long plackets and large armholes assure greater ease in dressing the baby.
2. Vanta garments avoid the use of pins.
3. Plenty of changes in all garments will aid in always keeping the baby clean and dainty, and will also save the mother worry if garments cannot be laundered at once.
4. Rubber pants should be worn only for special occasions.
5. Oblong diapers afford greater possibilities in folding in different sizes as the baby grows.
6. Stockings with tab ends for pinning to diaper or a loop of tape sewed to the top mean that pins do not tear the top of the stocking.
7. Buy the best quality of outing flannel for garments for it will wear longer.
8. Baby buntings are a necessity, for babies can be so easily and safely accustomed to out-of-doors naps when mothers are unable to take them out for airings. When made with sleeves they allow for more exercise and enjoyment for the baby and might easily be made into a coat later.
9. Twistless tape is satisfactory.
10. Bootees and shoes need a draw string around the ankle so they will stay on better.
11. Thumbless mittens are best for tiny hands.

www.ingramcontent.com/pod-product-compliance
Lightning Source LLC
Chambersburg PA
CBHW031619040426
42452CB00006B/590